BRASS TAX

14 actionable insights to power your success

Jared Dunkin

"If you can make one heap of all your winnings And risk it on one turn of pitch-and-toss, And lose, and start again at your beginnings, And never breathe a word about your loss..."

— Rudyard Kipling

CONTENTS

Prologue

The ideas in this book are intended to:

- Contain actionable and practical advice,

- be relevant at *any* level of an organization BUT especially focused on recent graduates entering the workforce, and

- be of sufficient length to develop meaningful, insightful points AND short enough to read on the train or bus to/from work

I was inspired to write the book to capture insights that came to me while managing an in-house corporate tax function at a global media company. The book quickly touched a chord with many folks, from entry-level college grads to leading CEOs, who wrote and welcomed these ideas as something fresh and helpful.

Written with the entry-level staff person in mind, the book deals with concepts which can loosely be organized in 3 buckets: (a) finding and creating opportunities, (b) communicating them upwards and across an organization, and (c) executing. I have not encountered other books covering precisely these topics, in an actionable and simple way.

Just a quick note about my specialty — as a tax lawyer, when structuring transactions you have to know where you're going, figure out how to get there with precision, and communicate complex plans to audiences ranging from the staff level to the boardroom. And when I was assigned management of non-tax functions, those skills served me well time and again, but the experiences outside of tax helped me better to appreciate how critical other factors are, including the ability to animate, influence, and inspire others!

In essence, the book is about how to make your unique contribution in today's corporate world.

1. Would you wear a bathing suit to a wedding? When is it cool to be hip?

A mentor taught me that we are as important as we make other people feel. How would you feel if a guest turned up at your wedding wearing a bathing suit?

Each day I am meeting with corporate and investment bankers, partners at law firms and accounting firms, senior management and my team. Depending on the meeting, I oscillate between being the adviser and being the client. When I am the adviser, I am mindful of my dress and the image I am projecting. When I am the client, I am mindful of the image the adviser is projecting.

Years ago, I used to work on long complex tax opinions and I will never forget the time when a senior partner called me into her office to point out mistakes in a few of the footnotes. She told me that although the technical analysis was perfect the sloppiness in the footnotes would make the client question the quality of the entire work. As Einstein said, "whoever is careless with the truth in small matters cannot be trusted with important matters."[1]

Advisers: your choice of clothing may seem like a small matter but it isn't — being appropriately dressed inspires confidence, thoughtfulness and seriousness. I know it is hard to find the right balance as being overdressed can sometimes seem as bad as being under-dressed. As Peggy Noonan recently wrote in the WSJ,"[i]t has to do with forgetting who you are. It has to do with refusing to be fully adult and neglecting to take on, each day, the maturity, grace and self-discipline that are expected of adults and part of their job.... [Don't wear] soft clothes, the kind 5-year-olds favor."[2]

A Yale study compared negotiations done while wearing sweats vs. suits and not surprisingly, the suits far outperformed the sweats.[3] The suits sent signal of success and confidence that had immediate and tangible results. Also, there has been a lot of research on the internal benefits of dressing up and the improvement it offers to abstract thinking.[4]

So where does this take us? How do you "dress for the client"? I think dressing for the client means making the client feel important. This is sometimes hard to figure out, so instead of trying to guess whether the client wants weekend casual or professional dress I suggest don't think too hard and just dress up. You may think dressing the same as your client will put them at ease, but that is a common mistake in the professional world. Remember, we are as important as we make other people feel.

2. Would you check your cell phone at a funeral? When is it cool to be old school?

"I'm only as good as my last word, my last hook, my last bridge."
- Kendrick Lamar[5]

Once a friend fêted me to a Kendrick Lamar concert and I was amazed by Lamar's consummate artistry. However, I was surprised and disturbed by the number of fans capturing the moment on their cell phones, rather than deeply listening. It made me realize the same problem exists in the corporate world.

In this chapter, I want to explore the right approach to having productive meetings and specifically cell phones.

A recent study found that the average person taps, pokes, pinches or swipes their personal phone two thousand six hundred seventeen times a day.[6] The temptation is obvious — all that the connected world has to offer, condensed into a small device that fits in the palm of one's hand and almost never leaves one's side. However, one fascinating study found that just having a phone in your pocket (without looking at it) drains your brain of energy and cognitive capacity — it actually reduces intelligence and attention span.[7] This is because we are only capable of processing a small amount of information at any given time. Research also shows it takes 20 minutes to create deep focus in conversation and every time we check our phones we have to restart.[8]

I understand at the Pentagon cell phones are not allowed resulting in much more effective and powerful meetings.[9] What is the proper balance?

Just as dressing properly both changes you and the importance you give to the other person across the table, there are many other intangible factors that contribute to a successful meeting. The key intangible is being "all in."[10] It is impossible to be "all in" when there are cell phones on the table. I frequently tell my team about the importance of being focused on what they are doing and how cell phones interfere with that.

One cannot stress too much the importance of making others feel you care, and paradoxically, the real human connections happen in the times between meetings when, unfortunately, most are checking their phones! Thus, by putting away your cell phone, you show that you are putting the needs of others before your own, and when you do this, counter intuitively, your needs get taken care of by the very people you put first.

3. Are you a "What's Up" or *WhatsApp* kind of person?

My late father taught me the invaluable lesson that in life every moment, every interaction, matters.

And Bob Dylan sings in *It's Alright, Ma*, "you're either busy being born, or you're busy dying."[11] Every moment is a crossroad that you can either use to affect others in a positive and inspiring way or not — there is no middle ground.

Research has shown that your workplace environment is one of the biggest factors contributing to satisfaction to work.[12] And at the end of the day, you create the environment you are in — all it costs is asking, 'what's up?'

Above, I wrote about the danger of cell phones to having effective interactions with others.[13] I received numerous comments expressing many different viewpoints, and now I want to take it a step further. It is not just about putting your cell phone away, it is about what you do afterwards — turning to the person sitting on your left and saying hello. It is impossible to do this while syncing up with your friends on *WhatsApp*.

I tell everyone on my team the power of 'what's up?' Adam Neumann, the co-founder of WeWork, once recounted how when he first came to America he was surprised by how infrequently people said 'hello.' As an experiment, every day for a month in the elevator he practiced saying an engaging hello, and by the end of the month the energy and fabric of the entire building had changed — in short, he helped to create a community. Adam's hello became the seed of a multibillion dollar enterprise that is changing the world, which shows that you never know where your hello will lead you.

Research shows that emotions can be transmitted through a network of people up to three degrees of separation away.[14] While we are undeniably reaching people through texts, tweets, posts, we are missing the human energy, limitless possibilities, and downright fun that only happen when you say hello. My late father was a successful businessman but in the end he is remembered most for his consistent, caring and curious 'what's up?'

4. Tyson, Einstein, or Littlefinger? 7 tips to nail a C-suite meeting!

Years ago at my first executive level presentation, the company's CFO looked over at me and asked "how's it going?" I am not sure why but I answered, "as the great sage Mike Tyson once said 'everyone has a plan until they get punched in the face.'"[15] They all laughed at this quip and we had a terrific meeting.

Leadership requires seeing and finding opportunities, communicating, and then executing on those opportunities. Presenting to management is a muscle that has to be constantly exercised and if you don't get to do it often (or even if you do) you should seek frequent opportunities to simulate the experience with colleagues.

This chapter dives into 7 tips on how to communicate to management. You likely know these already on a deeper level, but simply forget how effective they can be:

1. **The opening and taking a position** — you should memorize the first part of the presentation cold and tell it as an inviting story, oscillating between the macro and the micro with a clear agenda to follow. In addition, take a position and be willing to defend it. David Ogilvy, referred to by many as the father of advertising, said that there is no shortage of people with brains — however, "the spinal column seems to be in much shorter supply!"[16]

2. **Explain it simply** — as Einstein said "if you can't explain it simply, you don't understand it well enough."[17] Figure out a way to explain issues in a concise manner and leave out unnecessary points. Be comfortable sometimes living with ambiguity. Remember, we all have managers and all our managers have managers who have lots on their plate — when we don't do quality work up front to distill the true essence of our message our audience must spend 5 times more effort and time to get to the same place and in the end, decisions can't be made timely, or simply can't be made.

3. **The feeling** — the research shows that people forget the things you say but do not forget how you made them feel,[18] which provides another essential tool for more effective communication — prior to the meeting meditate on the feeling you want to leave your audience with. The information we convey is important but we interpret information based on our emotional situation at the time. Each person will have a different experience. Understanding the power you have as a presenter, including the unspoken manifestations that you create in the mind of your listeners, is critical — if you care about others' needs, and they can sense that care you can change the emotional

state of the entire room and leave people remembering the "why" of the meeting long after.

4. **Headspace of Superwoman/man** — it is easy to doubt yourself and your abilities before a big meeting. Remind yourself of the skills you bring to the table and why the organization trusted to put you there in the first place — you will find that your confidence grows to the level you need it to be. Also, I recommend that you watch this essential TED talk on posture and body language from Amy Cuddy, *Your body language may shape who you are*, and find out why you should "fake it until you *become* it...!"[19] Project confidence and you will find confidence while surrounding yourself with confident people also helps (it is contagious).

5. **Credibility** — if asked a question you don't know the answer to, it is OK to say "great question, I hadn't thought of that angle, let me get back to you on it" — you lose credibility when you try to "spin" your questioner. Also be strong and secure enough to sometimes say "no" and always manage expectations!

6. **The "dirt"** — In season 7 of Game of Thrones, Littlefinger advises Sansa, "Don't fight in the North or the South. Fight every battle everywhere, always, in your mind. Everyone is your enemy, everyone is your friend. Every possible series of events is happening all at once. Live that way and nothing will surprise you. Everything that happens will be something that you've seen before."[20] You need to be prepared to dig down into the dirt and answer questions 5 clicks down. In this regard, simulation is an indispensable tool — do not neglect it!

7. **Flow** — remember your agenda and at appropriate moments, guide the conversation back to the agenda, while having the judgment when not to do this. This is really hard and takes many years to grasp. Most people are unable to deviate from a planned presentation to follow the deeper underlying flow — where the conversation *should* go. The key is to know when and how to bring the conversation back to the agenda and when to let the conversation deviate.

Remember, presenting to management is a muscle that has to be continually exercised. The tips will work if you are self-aware, mindful and persistent.

5. Finding a diamond in a muddy road — what is your creative space to play?[21]

The Talmud says, "when you grasp for everything, you end up grasping for nothing."[22]

Do you ever feel confused and frustrated when trying to figure out your mandate at work while not annoying your boss or stepping on anyone's toes?

There is no better factory of personal and professional development than the workplace. Research shows that top performers are masters of selectivity — ruthlessly figuring out the priorities and tasks most needing their attention and then devoting strong and sustained efforts to accomplish them.

In the corporate world, this means finding opportunities, communicating them upward, and then executing. Above, I wrote about communicating through effective presentations, but this chapter is about executing by defining your "creative space to play" — really hard stuff.

One day, I met with a senior executive of a rapidly growing global company. I asked him how he manages to keep up with the tremendous growth of the company and execute on multiple initiatives. He told me, "I am so aligned with the leader's vision that I know my authority and the decision power I have... I then periodically check my past decisions with leadership to make sure I am continuously aligned."

While some people, like this executive, align intuitively with what their leaders wish to achieve, there are three elements that I believe each of us can use to find our creative space: (1) mindfulness, (2) self-awareness, and (3) determining one's responsibility.

Mindfulness allows one to develop and maintain a calm and focused attention necessary to move from a reactive to proactive mindset (check out Headspace, an app that has helped anchor me in the midst of my chaotic schedule).[23]

In addition, self-awareness is key — knowing yourself and how others perceive you. The reality is we overestimate how much we know about ourselves, and often we are afraid to get feedback to understand how we are experienced by others (just try asking people what they don't like about you!).

Lastly, you need to figure out your responsibility. The trick is to use mindfulness and self-awareness to meditate on all of your responsibilities — to your employer, your manager, your employees, your colleagues, and your customers. You will be amazed at how important these responsibilities are. And these will help you to define and discover your creative space to play at work and the mandate you have. The point is you define it... don't wait for someone else to do it for you.

As an added benefit, when you do this hard thinking up front, your check-ins with your manager will become quick, effective and smart — just a simple matter of determining if you are aligned. Harold Macmillan, the British statesman and former PM, when asked what was most likely to send his administration off course reputedly said "events, dear boy, events."[24] Of course, we are all buffeted by the craziness and force of events every day but with the above strategy you can find your creative space to play.

6. Sandcastles and Waves: 3 tips for finding the "art of the possible"

As mentioned in the Prologue, the subject matter of this book is intended to meet 3 conditions: (1) containing actionable and practicable advice, (2) relevant at any level of an organization, but especially focused on recent graduates entering the workforce, and (3) short enough to read on the train or bus to work, but long enough to develop meaningful and insightful points. The first 6 chapters of the book all relate to one or more of the following three buckets, all 3 of which you need to make it in the corporate world: (a) finding and creating opportunities, (b) communicating them upwards, and (c) executing.

So here's where we are — we have explored how to dress, being fully present while at work, how to engage your colleagues and lift them up, how to effectively present at meetings, and how to find your creative space to play.

In the last chapter about finding your creative space, I discussed the importance of mindfulness, self-awareness, and determining one's responsibility, which in some ways relates to "executing"; but finding one's creative space also requires one to be able to find and see opportunities. This chapter focuses on finding and seeing the opportunities.

• Don't self-assess

Charles Duhigg, in *The Power of Habit*[25] cites a Duke University study that found that more than 40 percent of the actions we perform each day are not actual decisions, but habits. Habits are choices that we deliberately make at some point, and then stop thinking about (but continue doing). Breaking a habit requires cognitive exertion, and may benefit from discussion with others. Companies have habits too so just because something is done a certain way, it doesn't mean that was a deliberate decision — or even if it was deliberate, that the decision can't be changed. Never self-assess why something 'can't' be done — present your team or boss with the art of the possible and get their agreement before deciding that it really can't be done. In my career, I have seen it happen over and over again where people decide that something can't be done and then never bring the possibility to management.

Even if you do bring the idea to management, the idea may not be accepted — however, at least it will be considered. As Steve Jobs said, "[p]eople think focus means saying yes to the thing you've got to focus on. But that's not what it means at all. It means saying no to the hundred other good ideas that there are. You have to pick carefully. I'm actually as proud of the things we haven't done as the things I have done. Innovation is saying no to 1,000 things."[26] By having presented the possibility at the right time, even if you are wrong at the end it means that your team will have made the best decision possible based on the information available at the time.

- **Be persistent and precise**

Rembrandt's brilliance was his precision — each strand of hair was painted individually. It was this extreme degree of control that facilitated his creativity.[27] At Amazon, employees are expected to draft a six-page narrative memo before each meeting, which is a recipe for better ideas. Slow thinking works.

Einstein said, "[i]t's not that I'm so smart, it's just that I stay with problems longer."[28] Creativity is a child of discomfort. Stay with something for a long time and try to make connections between disparate things. I have been amazed how, when I just plant an idea in my head and stop thinking about it for some time the answer will suddenly hit me.

The answer may come while you are in the shower or when you wake up in the morning. However, somewhat counter-intuitively, I find that I am most creative when practicing the discipline of putting pen to paper — through specific and precise description of what the problem is.

- **Avoid ghosting — even at the cost of discomfort!**

I understand that in the dating world there is a phenomenon called 'ghosting' — this happens when a person suddenly cuts off all communication with another person that they were previously interacting with, without warning. I have started noticing that this occurs in the corporate world as well, where people ignore direct questions and emails. But no response is a response — just another kind. Remember that discomfort is imperative. By ghosting, you lose trust that can't be regained; in addition, by avoiding a difficult conversation early on you simply make the same conversation even more difficult later on, and prevent creativity by keeping the situation locked in the status quo.

By forcing yourself not to ghost you make sure you and others will see and create opportunities at the right time.

Conclusion

If you do the above 3 things, you will find and see new opportunities in your daily work. Of course, the starting point is to enter the game without ever being satisfied (as Edison said, "show me a thoroughly satisfied man and I will show you a failure"[29]). You need to wake up each day and consistently worry that someone else might make a better contribution than you — this will ensure that you continuously stretch yourself and contribute to the world in ways others cannot. And this is also the key to happiness.

7. How many doors do you see? The joy of what can be...

Nobel Laureate Daniel Kahneman, in his best-selling book T*hinking, Fast and Slow*[30] explains that there is "fast thinking" and "slow thinking". Fast thinking is the innate sense to the answer of a problem (e.g., 2+2=?), whereas slow thinking requires concentration and analysis. The problem is slow thinking is oft times not employed long enough and hard enough to catch the errors of intuitive fast thinking or to help us make the right decision in cases where fast thinking just doesn't work.

In his 2015 letter to shareholders, Jeff Bezos wrote about the problem of knowing when to do slow thinking versus fast thinking.[31] I've previously written about how Amazon requires employees to draft a six-page narrative memo before each meeting (clearly a company that emphasizes the value of slow thinking); but Bezos distinguishes between "one-way doors" and "two-way doors." He described making the mistake of treating some decisions as one-way doors which slowed down the decision making process — leading to "slowness, unthoughtful risk aversion, failure to experiment sufficiently, and consequently diminished invention." In fact, most doors are two-way doors, meaning "you can walk through the door, and walk back through to the other side if it isn't working." If it is a two-way door, then the corollary is that you can make it with 70% of the information and still be okay with that — not letting the perfect become the enemy of the good.

The key is simply knowing what type of decision you are making — and knowing when to slow down to apply the right slow thinking to the problem because it actually is a one-way door.

However, after you enter either the one-way or two-way door there is also a "third door" that not everyone sees. My initial inspiration about this third door came from reading Alex Banayan's eponymous book, *The Third Door*[32] Banayan interviewed celebrities and industry moguls to identify the secret to their success, and weaves a compelling narrative about the role of innate curiosity and ability to foray into areas where others simply don't tread, as key traits defining an individual's success.

Building further on Banayan's idea, what I refer to as the "third door" is a portal that leads you to unexpected places and exponential growth and opportunity. This third door is a state of mind relating to how we view our actions and requires remembering that every moment can be a "magic moment."

The third door exists in your every day, and in the commonplace activities you do that may not seem so magical or of supreme importance. This can be easy to forget. Because by definition, the third door is hidden.

By finding (and visualizing) this third door, those of us who work in corporate functions can have magic moments where we discover new savings in cash or in time, provide greater certainty and clarity to our executives, and — here comes the most important part of all — do what it takes to enable our colleagues and our teams to discover their own magic moments.

I tell my team: imagine the feeling you'll have when that happens (you create a magic moment) and take that feeling into the now to energize yourself and everything you do. Most people think that a magic moment requires you to already have achieved some remarkable result (sense of pride and accomplishment) — not so.

A few more ideas that may help you to unlock your third door. First, vulnerability — allow yourself to do it. Mistakes happen so when they do, don't condemn others or yourself — take responsibility and understand and grow from it. Second, enter whatever you do with energy — understand the value of speed and completion and a belief in the importance of what you are doing. Third, remember every day is an adventure and that work can and should be fun.

8. Are you adulting? Churchill vs. the sycophants

I randomly met a former captain in the Navy (the power of What's Up?). I asked him what was the biggest shock going from the Navy to corporate world and surprisingly he said the number of sycophants in the latter. The captain said at the top ranks in the Navy, you are there to tell your commanding officer what they don't know — they don't need you to tell them what they already know.

As a manager of a lean team, part of my mentoring strategy is to make my team comfortable to tell me what I don't know — it is because of this my team has become so high achieving that one can say: "never was so much owed by so many to so few."[33] We all have to do more with less. And the key is contribution, not numbers. In making a contribution numbers don't count — what matters is commitment, energy, dedication. In physics, applying a massive amount of pressure to an object collapses its molecules and changes the nature of the object. A lean team feels this pressure and undergoes a transformation. Less is more!

The secret that my team gets is how important it is to focus on their contribution to the company, each other and our collective story. This is because they are not entitled and see the role they play as a responsibility.

So who are the people you should hire to help you do this?

My life mentor[34] taught me how. He pointed out that there are experienced and tenured people at companies who appear better candidates than younger and inexperienced folks. He acknowledged that while experience and tenure can sometimes root one's thinking in the past, lack of experience can impair judgment. However, instead of classifying people according to this faulty dichotomy, he said the key to a good hire is figuring out if they have the quality of "adulthood," which has little to do with age and more to do with being resilient, humble, and a life-long learner.

9. The importance of being Marvin — 3 tips for unlocking your potential

"A diamond is just a lump of coal that stuck to its job."

- Leonardo da Vinci[35]

While waiting in line for a kosher hot dog at the U.S. Open, I noticed a worker in an adjacent stand making soft salted pretzels without wearing gloves. A tourist and I looked at each other in disgust when all of a sudden the gentleman behind me shouts to the worker's manager, "hey — shouldn't he be wearing gloves? this isn't right!" He then looked at us and explained, "this is NY, when you see something that is not right, you shout!" Chutzpah.

Moments later I got my hot dog and the cashier told me the credit card machine isn't working. I said, I don't have cash. Next thing I know, Mr. Chutzpah pulled out $20 bill and said, "here you go, I am Marvin." I asked him, how can I repay you, and he replied, "I will be sitting somewhere over there, in the sea of people." Generosity.

Social capital[36] is the concept that a society's wealth is more than just money — it involves trust within a society and knowing that folks care about you and will help you in a time of need and tell you when things are wrong. Folks like Marvin.

And the glue to all this is slowing down and noticing folks around you, and caring — we are all under tremendous pressure (both at work and with other things that happen to us in life) and so it is frequently hard to stop and do what is right.

Marvin taught me that we should never be too much in a rush to stop and invest our time in others; we can all use more kindness.

- **But how do we DO what Marvin does? — the key is overcoming indifference...**

Elie Wiesel said, "[t]he opposite of love is not hate, it's indifference"[37] — we live in world of incredible turmoil and it is so easy to fall prey to indifference. We become unaware of our insensitivity.

Discomfort is the key to change.

Discomfort gives us an avenue to overcome that innate tendency — when we are uncomfortable, it makes us work to change the situation. Discomfort can sometimes be created by things like loss of a job, the onset of an illness, or the death of a loved one. However, we can also create discomfort by reflecting on the gap between where we are and where we want to be.

3 ideas to help you reflect on how to close the gap between where you are and where you want to be:

1. **Reflect on what can be** — in chapter 7, I discussed the concept of "one-way" and "two-way" doors — those that are reversible and those that aren't. And after you enter this door that there is also a "third door" that not everyone sees and leads you to unexpected places and exponential growth and opportunity. The ticket in is vulnerability, commitment, courage and adventure. I began reflecting on the doors I never entered in life — the "could-have-beens" and "might-have-beens" that did not come to be. A frequent underlying reason for not entering one's third door is fear of failure. So, be mindful of that and meditate on the pain of losing out on what could be — this is a powerful tool that you can use to propel yourself forward into action. As Wayne Gretzky puts it, "you always miss 100% of the shots you don't take!"[38]

2. **Do more** — a prominent man once came to Rabbi Menachem Schneerson, the late Chabad-Lubavitch leader from Crown Heights, and said he was holding down three full time jobs and it all seemed too much for one person and so asked the rabbi what he should focus on. The rabbi instructed that he should continue to do all the things he was already doing, and to do more things and work even harder. The rabbi believed that by doing more, one would change the very nature of reality and exceed the limits of the human condition. It is when we dig down deep inside the dirt, that we find diamonds. And it is a principle from physics that when one applies massive amounts of

pressure to an object, the molecules collapse and the very nature of the object changes (and this is how diamonds are formed out of carbon). Hustling and doing more both require putting the needs of others before our own and when we do this, counter-intuitively, our needs get taken care of precisely by the people we put first.

3. **Give rather than take** — in Adam Grant's important book, *Give and Take*[39] he explains there are 3 types of people — givers, takers and what he calls "matchers". Grant defines givers as people who "help others without expecting anything in return"; takers, as those who "like to get more than what they give"; and matchers, as those who "help others to get back equally". Adam finds that givers are more likely to succeed than takers. The challenge is that some takers disguise themselves as givers and one way to spot their true colors is by the type of behavior captured in the Dutch phrase, "kissing up, kicking down". And this is the point of self-reflection — what are you really? Are you giving strategically, like a matcher, because you expect something in return, or just giving? The life-changing idea is that by just giving, we are helping someone do something, just for its own sake — having this singular dedication, during the moments of service to the people that one serves, and even subordinating one's self-interest to theirs during that process, is the key to getting it right. And through all this, one must be mindful that even if one is a natural giver, one can still find oneself deviating from that tendency because of one's emotional situation at any given particular moment in time.

As Paolo Coelho put it, "you must be the person you have never had the courage to be. Gradually, you will discover that you are that person, but until you can see this clearly, you must pretend and invent."[40]

Even if we aren't yet like Marvin, we can remake ourselves to be more like him. In *Rich Boy* by Sharon Pomerantz[41] the author explores the protagonist's complex relationship with his working class family in the post-war years. The novel takes an unexpected twist when Robert brings home a sophisticated wealthy British girlfriend not knowing what to expect. Robert is shocked when she tells him, "you have it all wrong about them." She shares her view with him about his family — his mother wasn't cheap but a brilliant home economist, his father imaginative and literary, and his brother so much like him. She remade them all. The family senses how she remade them and like seeing themselves through her eyes.

We humans are not just made out of carbon molecules — similar to carbon, you need to see us in the right light to realize our potential to be diamonds. If you are able to use the above techniques to overcome your indifference, you can become a diamond.

10. Autonomy vs. Accountability — solving the Rubik's Cube....

"When you're 20 you care what everyone thinks,
when you're 40 you stop caring what everyone thinks,
when you're 60 you realize no one was ever thinking
about you in the first place."

- Winston Churchill[42]

The secret to being a great leader or employee is simply to behave as the leader you wish to follow and the employee you love to manage.

But how do you do this?

As an initial matter, you have to know which 'hat' you are wearing — sometimes you are manager and other times employee — it is always changing. Be mindful of this — it matters!

It matters because autonomy and accountability often appear to be in conflict with one another. However, autonomy is a leadership style while accountability is a character trait, and the two are innately interrelated. This chapter will give you practical tips on how to use accountability as the currency for achieving the autonomy that you (or your employee) need to be successful.

Steve Jobs said, "it doesn't make sense to hire smart people and tell them what to do; we hire smart people so they can tell us what to do."[43] Autonomy is a leadership style — hire smart people and let them tell you what you don't know. This requires hiring employee who are capable of "adulting."[44] Moreover, the reality of today is that our jobs are so specialized that your manager likely can't do your job and doesn't know what you do on a daily basis.

So what do you do when you provide autonomy to your employees and have this nagging feeling something is off or you are an employee and your manager doesn't give you the autonomy you seek? This happens when the employee lacks accountability — a character trait. However, it is a character trait that can be learned. Remember Marvin and how we can learn and improve from our daily interactions.[45]

Accountability requires communicating upward, being transparent, and generating trust. If your manager has to wonder what you are doing, that is a problem. If your manager has to ask where something is, that is a problem. If you think something is happening because you had a couple meetings, but nothing else is emerging from those meetings, or if you are just waiting for your manager to take your work and drive it through, that reflects possible naiveté and could also be a problem.

Conversely, when things are going well, it means your employees are communicating upward and so aligned with your vision that they can execute on multiple initiatives in a harmonious manner.

This is all well and good, but, how do you actually achieve this level of accountability in practice?

For my part, having reached an age when I am supposed to "not care what everyone thinks", I pretend like I am a 60-year old (as Churchill says, "no one was ever thinking about [me]") — meaning that I am empowered to be autonomous. But simultaneously, I am also a 20-year old! Which means that like a 20-year old, I constantly worry whether my manager knows what I am doing and care what they think about me. I realize that it is challenging to push many things through because of numerous competing priorities facing you and your team, however, the only way to cut through all of this is to meditate daily about what needs to get done.

Another way to think about your situation is to meditate on your manager's stress, and realize that if you worry about communicating properly (the 20-year old), that will help you get the support you need to drive things through (the 60-year old).

The attitude that ties all of these together can be described as "urgency plus care."

11. *"I would have written a shorter email, but I did not have the time!"* — the secret to decision making

We have discussed often about the "what" and the "who" of decisions — those you are empowered to make, and figuring out the balance between autonomy and accountability. We have also spoken about how to meditate on your responsibilities to define and discover your creative space to play at work because as the Talmud says, "when you grasp for everything, you end up grasping for nothing."

We have also discussed the imperative to make decisions — whether reversible (a/k/a "Two-Way Doors") or not — as Andy Grove used to say about decisions, "you have to make them when you have to make them."

But what if you are not the decision maker — what can you do to move the ball forward? There is a great scene in Downton Abbey where the Earl of Grantham says to Matthew, "We all have different parts to play, Matthew, and we should all be allowed to play them." The key is to recognize that all of us every day are either involved in decisions, or managing up to others who need to make decisions.

There is something that you can do immediately, at any level of an organization, and which (if you get it right) will become the linchpin to your success — simply, make a daily practice of facilitating good decision-making by putting yourself in the shoes of the decision maker, and using that perspective to inform everything you do. This requires humility to understand what your role really is and empathy. Remember that decision makers are often beset with way too much information and often don't get the full picture till the last minute. That is where you come in.

In the modern workplace, where the average person checks email 74 times a day and switches tasks on computer 566 times a day, and needs to touch between 10 to 20 people per day just to get their job done, the task of filtering the endless information and figuring out what decision needs to be made is close to impossible. Multiply this by the complexity of global business and constant attention-shifting, and the decision maker's task becomes even more of a challenge.

A good friend of mine who was a senior official in a recent administration told me he trained his staff to draft short bullet-point memos — he described them as "well-conceived, comprehensive but succinct, plain English background papers" and used to assimilate vast amounts of information on his 7 minute commute to meet the President. I find this a helpful way to think about emails or slide decks — tools that present the right information starkly and can facilitate the best possible decision-making, at the right time.

This means that, when action is needed, you need to be able to summarize all the relevant and critical information (usually stored in multiple long email chains) in a way that can be brought to the decision makers in a digestible and concise format. You are adding tremendous value when you have provided the decision maker everything they need to make an informed decision.

It is extremely satisfying that when you get it right and play your role the decision maker can do their job. A leader I used to work for, Tom Monahan, called this the "tennis match of ideas" — with leader serving as an umpire who can stop the ball in the air and ask, "this looks like the best idea — how much would it be worth if we got this really right?"[46]

12. Superhuman Fuel: Recognizing the Good

"I feel a very unusual sensation — if it is not indigestion,
I think it must be gratitude."
- Benjamin Disraeli

We all know extraordinary people who make us wonder, 'how is it that they can juggle and accomplish so many things? And how is it that have they achieved such a deep level of happiness?' I believe it is because these individuals understand the tremendous power of responsibility, and the limitlessness of gratitude[47] — the fuel for achieving superhuman results.

In a prior chapter,[48] we talked about how happiness comes from figuring out your responsibility in the world (to your employer, your manager, your employees, your colleagues, and your customers) and contributing to the world in that way that only you can. The trick is to use mindfulness and self-awareness to meditate on all your responsibilities, which will help you to find your creative space to play. In addition, doing so in a way that permits you to stretch yourself and contribute to the world in ways that others cannot is the key to fulfillment. For as Victor Frankl said, "success, like happiness, cannot be pursued; it must ensue, and it only does so as the unintended side-effect of one's personal dedication to a cause greater than oneself."[49]

Gratitude creates another form of responsibility to others — a sense of indebtedness to and appreciation of those around you. The research shows that these types of emotions are a key driver of lasting happiness.[50]

Gratitude improves physical, mental, psychological and social health, as shown in a famous Harvard longitudinal study, summarized in this TED talk by Robert Waldinger titled *'What makes a good life; lessons from the longest study on happiness'.*[51]

According to Waldinger, 3 top takeaways from the happiness study are that:

> Social connections are really good for us, for both our physical and mental wellbeingit's not just the number of friends you have (and I'm not talking Facebook!), but the quality of each of those connections, and the happiest folks are those who "leaned into" their relationships — at work, with family, and with their community.

Recently we experienced the joy of bringing a new baby boy into the world. It amazed me how many people leaned in to support us — my four daughters, family, friends, community, colleagues, and others. When we adopt a mindset of gratitude we begin to see how much kindness is being done to us, and can appreciate the beauty of friendships, good health, and jobs — and also just the "everyday stuff". Jennifer B. Wallace has written in the Wall Street Journal about the importance of gratitude, and of finding ways to open kids' eyes to and helping them appreciate the everyday stuff.[52]

But first, back to those extraordinary people, the ones with seemingly-supernatural ability and truly superhuman accomplishments — my contention is that the reason they can achieve so much is they realize the true question isn't how "big" the task before them is — rather the real question has to do with figuring out their "Responsibility" to the world. And when I say "Responsibility," I mean that one responsibility in the world that is solely yours, that only you can do and **no one else can do for you.**

This Responsibility is created by many factors but nothing contributes to it more than the indebtedness that you have to others for the kindness that they have shown you. The secret is that because you were the beneficiary of the kindness, you have become specially responsible vis-à-vis the kindness and are the only person who can now repay it. This creates a powerful energy and provides one with the "fuel" to achieve the truly superhuman...

Here are **3 tips** for cultivating gratitude as a daily practice:

1. **Ask for help:** it takes courage to ask for help, because saying 'thank you' means acknowledging that you needed the other person. But remember, firstly that people want to give to you, and that by asking for their help, you are

giving them the chance to contribute to your success (so long as they don't feel taken advantage of), and secondly, that only through others can you fill up your "fuel box" to achieve those superhuman results

2. **Remove your ego:** it blinds us and causes us to put ourselves and our own rights ahead of anyone else, living a self-centered existence that is the antithesis of happiness and eventually leads to the loneliness that Waldinger discusses in his TED Talk, which kills.[53] The ego doesn't want to acknowledge its own debt to others... but saying 'thank you' creates humility and is a powerful tool in ego diminishment. Gratitude requires a recognition of tremendous kindness others have done for us, and acknowledges the open question of how we can adequately repay it...

3. **Say thank you and be specific as to why:** a good exercise is to set a daily calendar reminder each morning for 2 minutes to stop and meditate on particular act of kindness done by someone else for you (or for someone close to you) — ask yourself in the second person, "what are you grateful for?" (I've noticed that using the second person avoids the ego implicit in asking oneself "what am I grateful for?" and is an effective trick for getting out of the prison of "me"). Pause and feel the gratitude, and then write the person a short note, or find some other tangible way to express your gratitude. **Be very specific on what the person did beyond just saying a generic 'thank you'**

A genuine thank you is one currency we can use to repay our indebtedness. The best is if we can do so without waiting until someone does something, but finding things they have done already and demonstrating the gratitude enthusiastically. Remember — the research shows that grateful people tend to have better relationships, and that saying 'thank you' is a major factor in strengthening resilience, elicits better performance from employees, and enhances your relationships and friendships.

We cannot function without one another's help and support, we need each other and need to be able to admit it — it is important that we are clear in our minds about this. When people do help us, it is equally important that we show them abundant gratitude. It's the expression of that gratitude that unleashes their help, and which will unleash you to do things you can't even believe and find your Third Door.[54]

13. Kindness — costs nothing and wins you everything

"If you want people to think you are wise,
agree with them."

– Yiddish saying

Wisdom is achieved by asking oneself after daily interactions in what way the experience (positive or negative) has given you something that can improve your life. When you do this you transform the information or event into insights and wisdom.

As John Lennon said, "life happens when you're busy making other plans."[55] As we get older, life events come and go and we learn so many things (professionally and personally) – but unless we are extremely thoughtful, we may fail to apply the lessons we have spent a lifetime accumulating. On the other hand, if we pay attention to life and are mindful, we can use these insights and daily interactions to grow and make everything around us better.

Entering into 2019, I decided I wanted to explore those areas where "just because I can doesn't mean I should" – let me explain what I mean.

After college I was a Peace Corps volunteer in the Dominican Republic, and each morning a delivery man, affectionately called "Gordo" would visit the office where I worked to bring the newspaper, always balancing a large stack on his head. Gordo had extremely limited means, but he always entered the office with positivity, happiness and exuberantly excited at the sheer possibility of what can be. When you meet someone who is real you remember them forever – ever since those days, I have kept Gordo's spirit in mind and emulated him. I try to come to work each day positive, happy and exuberantly excited about what we are doing – and through kindness, I try to pass this along to my colleagues and team.

Herb Kelleher, co-founder and former CEO of Southwest Airlines, who passed away in the first days of 2019, said that the secret to his company's success was putting employees first. He tried to always remember their names and birthdays, made them feel valued, and entrusted them with important problems to solve.[56] Blake Nordstrom, the former co-president of Nordstrom, Inc. (who sadly passed away a day before Kelleher), was remembered by a septuagenarian former customer who once called the company to complain about a new billing format – she was surprised when he answered the phone, solved her issue, and took a continuing interest in her as a customer, which eventually led them to become friends.[57]

In another example of what I am saying, Doug Conant, former Campbell Soup CEO, famously hand-wrote 30,000 personal letters to his employees (up to 20 notes a day). He would re-count how he felt when he first arrived at the demoralized and ailing soup-maker. After years of meeting with employees and treating each as an important "touch point" of his day, he successfully turned the company around.[58] (A couple CEOs I worked for wrote me personal letters which I still proudly keep on my desk as they continue to motivate me.)

These are examples of great people and leaders who you would expect to have no time to deal with trifling matters of "unimportant" persons – but in fact, they showed their brilliance and their greatness precisely in these small moments of kindness, compassion, and empathy.

Good things are things worth doing in and of themselves; however, they usually have knock-on effects which are also positive. For example, Jeff Bezos has discussed how frugality (one of Amazon's 14 leadership principles) is good not only for budgeting purposes, but because it causes employees to cultivate resourcefulness, self-sufficiency, and capability for invention[59] In the same way, treating others with respect, dignity, and care (in a word, civility) will have important, beneficial side-effects for us in our everyday life and work.

It all comes down to how you make someone feel. Christine Porath has a wonderful TED Talk discussing the fact that civility really is a choice – that either you treat others with respect and dignity, make them feel valued, appreciated and heard; or you hold them down by making them feel small, disregarded, or excluded.[60] Moreover, because emotions can be transmitted through a network of people up to three degrees of separation away,[61] the end result is that incivility quantifiably reduces morale and performance throughout a network of people, like a contagion. Her research showed that civility was both associated with better team performance, and with leadership effectiveness – it is a virtuous circle.

Here are a few actionable things you can do every day:

1. Say hello! Greet others with a smile and a kind word. Try always being the first to reach out and say hello – this is a powerful way to make others feel good – and like Gordo, or these great leaders, you will have an outsized contribution and others will remember you for many years to come

2. Really listen! Listening means hearing the person, empathizing and letting them feel heard – it's not always about responding with a solution

3. Delegate and give space to execute! As Mr. Kelleher perfected, entrust your team and colleagues with important problems to solve and let them do their job. Even though you may be able to do their job better doesn't mean you should

4. Be grateful! Remember the superhuman power of gratitude to fuel it all[62]

Bottom line is you are either lifting people up, or holding them down. Every moment is a crossroad that you can either use to affect others in a positive and inspiring way or not — there is no middle ground.

14. *"See you later alligator!"* — how to win 20 Grand Prix races simultaneously

"It is amazing what you can accomplish if you do not care who gets the credit." - Harry Truman

An old boss of mine liked to say, "if you're wrestling an alligator, it's better to be on top." When you enter an American bookstore today, you will encounter more shelves of books devoted to leadership, management, and allied topics than to almost anything else, but I believe 84% of everything you need to know to be an effective manager and leader involves wrestling with one thing — your **ego** (scarier than any alligator I've seen!).[63]

The ego is not "bad" — it is absolutely necessary for us to do many things and maybe it even helps us to build the world. But like anything the ego needs to be regulated — we need to know how to keep it in check and remain mindful of it. This is because when it is unbalanced it can become unhealthy.

As a quick litmus test we can ask ourselves whether our self-esteem comes primarily from within, or whether it is primarily dependent on the opinion of others. Unfortunately, the need for honor, praise, and recognition increases the more these are pursued, and eventually it becomes insatiable. Persons craving respect and recognition will end up pursuing these things at the cost of their prime missions — and thus, the ego will get in the way of exercising effective leadership.

Our self-esteem comes from within and is healthy when we understand our responsibilities — previously described as our "Responsibility" to serve others and the benefit of gratefully acknowledging our indebtedness to others.[64] The key is to appreciate that it is not all about **YOU**, but rather, that you just happen to be the vehicle to fulfill this great Responsibility and thus, to repay your indebtedness to others. The more we work on this Responsibility, the stronger our healthy self-esteem becomes, and the less likely we are to be held hostage to the rapacious demands of an unchecked ego.

So how do you **DO** this?

Here are **8 tips** you may want to try out:

1. **Oprah Winfrey, *on keeping in mind the natural question, "how did I do?"*** — I once heard Oprah discuss her observation that, among the many celebrities and heads of state she has interviewed, at the end of an interview, their nearly invariable reaction was to turn around and ask the interviewer, *"how did I do?"* This is a telling reminder that,

no matter how far we go in life, the temptation to ask others "how am I doing" and seek out flattery can be irresistible[65] — but you may be helped simply by keeping this in mind and noting that the ego may be triggered in the process

2. **Don Fernando, *on cutting open coconuts*** — as a Peace Corps volunteer in the Dominican Republic years ago, I had the opportunity to encounter Don Fernando, a wealthy landowner and former revolutionary who had headed a strike force of women guerrillas against the right-wing dictatorship in 1959.[66] Don Fernando would often take me to visit his acres of breathtaking oceanfront property. He had numerous families living on and taking care of his land on his behalf (locally these folks are referred to as *"campesinos"*). I observed Don Fernando repeatedly going into their little shacks, pulling out a machete and personally cutting open fallen coconuts for their children to enjoy the fresh juice, all the while speaking to their parents about their lives and the goings-on in the land. And here's the rub: I later learned that Don Fernando actually grew up *himself* as a *campesino* and acquired all this land very slowly, over time. He once confessed to me that he never wanted to forget where he came from, and that by visiting the *campesinos* and cutting open the coconuts for them to drink, it reconnected him with his roots and helped him to remain grounded in the right feelings and perspectives[67]

3. **Arthur Blank, *on putting on the apron*** — Arthur Blank, the co-founder of Home Depot and owner of Atlanta Falcons, told WSJ that when he ran Home Depot he tried to spend up to half his time in his stores wearing an orange apron. He said, "if you're really willing to subordinate your

feelings to what the people you're serving are telling you, they'll be honest with you."[68] Of course few of us own large stores and are able to work the aisles at will, but we can think of what our business is and find our own ways to humble ourselves in order to connect with our employees and customers

4. **Adam Neumann, *on completely disconnecting 1 day per week*** — the co-founder of WeWork recently shared that when his company's valuation hit $5b (now valued at ~$47b), he noticed that he became unable to control his ego and began to automatically judge others and assume that he was better. However, Adam eventually understood that if you think you are better than others you become incapable of helping or leading them. He decided to disconnect completely from technology for 24 hours each week in order to connect with his family and friends and focus on spiritual matters ("why we are here and what is it all about")[69] — this helped him to remember to treat everyone as equals and continue to value the unique role that each person plays in the organization. I have witnessed the unique team culture that has arisen because of Adam's insight first hand and the respect, passion, generosity and trust Adam's team embodies is magical and enviable

5. **Lady Gaga, *on remembering who you are*** — Lady Gaga, or Steffani Germanotta in real life, has remarked that her public persona "Gaga" is a creation, different form herself and as she put it, a "separate entity from me."[70] This makes sense because our persona is an image that we show to others; the word comes from *'persona'* in Latin, in which language it originally referred to a theatrical mask through which the actor's voice passed and

was heard by the audience.[71] Sometimes in life or in our work, acting a particular role separate from our identity is an important responsibility, but at the end of the day, we must remember who we are, and Lady Gaga's existence depends on her remembering that she is actually Steffani Germanotta

6. **Tom Brady, *on making introductions*** — it is reported that Tom Brady, the star quarterback of the Patriots (sometimes referred to as the greatest quarterback in NFL history) greets all new players on the team by tapping them on the shoulder and saying "Hi, I'm Tom Brady."[72] Clearly, they know he is Tom Brady. And Brady understands that; but his introduction reflects awareness that everyone on the team has a role to play and that in this regard all team members are equals and are given the space to grow and succeed

7. **Andy Puddicombe, *on finding 10 minutes each day*** — Puddicombe helps us to focus on the fact that as we live in a frantic world in which our mind is our "most precious and most valuable resource," we end up spending so much time outside the present moment and out of touch with ourselves; in his TED Talk, Puddicombe relates how certain difficult events in his life led him to appreciate mindfulness[73] Mindfulness teaches us to live in the present moment and let go of the story-lines that the ego creates and thrives upon (or at least, to observe them without getting caught up in them). Mindfulness can best be improved through the exercise of meditation, and is about observing thoughts coming and going, and cultivating a different perspective on them. By meditating and increasing your mindfulness, you will not only remain present in the moment but will avoid getting caught up in the "story-lines"

that the ego creates (also check out *Headspace*, an app that Puddicombe pioneered, which helps me to stay calm and proactive in my busy schedule each day)[74]

8. **Amy Cuddy, *on posture and presence*** — in her refreshing and widely discussed TED Talk, Amy Cuddy discusses how "our bodies change our minds . . . and our minds change our behavior"[75]; while her talk focuses on the power of one's posture, Cuddy also points out that even more central is the feeling of *presence* that an individual brings to a room or a meeting, that makes others desire to connect with them — based on human qualities like authenticity, confidence, passion, and enthusiasm (of which factors posture is just a correlate), which in the end are the true drivers in how a person connects with others around them, and help to determine how the person makes us feel

An illustrious and renowned tax lawyer and mentor, Glen Kohl, mentioned to me that he views his job as simultaneously engaging in 20 *Grand Prix* races; if these races were all about him, he confessed he might win just 1 in 20, but would certainly lose the other 19; however, because he sees his job as being to always put the needs of his team and employer first, he is able to make sure that all 20 races are won.[76]

When we remember to put the needs of the company (and others) first and focus on these things instead of on ourselves and our own narrow self-interest, we can continuously stretch ourselves and contribute to the world in way that no one else can, and we propel our teams, our colleagues and our companies forward. As we discussed in a prior chapter, the brilliance of some individuals is revealed in the smallest moments of kindness, compassion, and empathy. And the door to that brilliance is humility.

Try out these tips out and let me know how it goes... when you remember these things, I hope you are able to use them to "fill the unforgiving minute / [w]ith sixty seconds' worth of distance run"[77] and that when sighting an alligator, you remember to say with a big smile, "see you later, alligator!"

Epilogue

There are certain qualities that are very difficult to write about, because they are simply 'great'. As Kazuo Ishiguro writes on the topic of English butlers in *The Remains of the Day*,

> You will notice I say 'what' rather than 'who' is a great butler; for there was actually no serious dispute as to the identity of the men who set the standards amongst our generation. . . . . If you have ever had the privilege of meeting such men, you will no doubt know of the quality they possess to which I refer. But you will no doubt also understand what I mean when I say it is not at all easy to define just what this quality is.[78]

Ishiguro makes the further point that figuring out who is great, and appreciating *what* makes them great requires a high degree of **discernment**. Similar to the great butlers Ishiguro describes, we have the opportunity in our lives to meet extraordinary people who impress us and leave us with a sense of childlike wonder; they may appear to have qualities we can only ape after, and we are grateful simply for the chance to meet them or work and be in their presence.

As a friend and mentor once told me, it is important to meditate each day on the leader one wishes one had, and on the employee one wishes one could manage. Like all the other suggestions in this book (including regularly expressing gratitude), that has to be a daily practice.[79]

In this book, I have attempted to trace a path that can help you find your own way to greatness in your professional life. In the prologue, I loosely grouped the concepts or "building blocks" of this approach under 3 major buckets: (a) finding and creating opportunities, (b) communicating them upwards, and (c) executing. In the course of investigating these ideas further, additional wrinkles and nuances appeared. For example, it is often in the course of articulating information for our manager (chapter 11) that we discover new opportunities (chapter 7).

In due course, I also noted certain themes and overarching principles. Take, for example, **discomfort** (a character trait we discussed in chapter 9 which can help you stretch yourself each day, and which you cultivate when you meditate on "the gap between where we are and where we want to be"), **responsibility** and **gratitude** (discussed in chapter 12, which will help you find your creative space to play), and **kindness** (chapter 13, which costs you nothing and wins you everything).

Practicing these principles can enable you to achieve truly superhuman results. And always make a habit of looking out for that third door which exists in your every day, in the commonplace activities that may not seem magical or critical, but which are of supreme importance!

A great person once said that all beginnings are difficult, and that makes sense because a beginning is half of everything.[80] By implementing the tools in this book, you will have made an important beginning.

Bonus Material

We are always oscillating between being the adviser and being the client (internally and externally) – here are some tips I wrote years ago on being a good client or being a good adviser. It is written for tax advisers but applicable to all professionals.

Article 1

Head Games: Tips for Getting Into the Head of Your Client

Each morning I go to Starbucks and order a grande caffe misto in a vente cup; for $2.50 I leave with a wonderful cup of coffee but more importantly I leave enriched by the experience.

The dignity and respect I receive not only impacts me but, indirectly, impacts the people I interact with throughout the day, including tax advisers.

The best of advisers, like the barista at Starbucks, leave me not only with a great product but a feeling of dignity and respect. They excite and stimulate me. The worst of them, however, leave me drained of energy and with the terrible feeling that I have been beguiled. Most advisers fall somewhere in the middle.

It was not until recently that I discovered how deceived I was in thinking I had uncovered the secrets to getting into the head of the client.

Prior to becoming the "client," I worked in the national office mergers and acquisitions group at a Big Four accounting firm. My clients were both internal and external. I spent a considerable amount of time trying to get into the head of my clients. Because I kept busy and remained consistently in demand, I figured I had successfully uncovered the secrets to client satisfaction.

It was not until recently, when I left the accounting firm to join the tax department at a large media company, that I discovered how deceived I was in thinking I had uncovered the secrets to getting into the head of the client. With that, I humbly put together a wish list for my advisers.

The following suggestions are not designed to teach you what you do not know, but rather to remind you of what you already know. It is due to forgetfulness, business, and pressures that we do not do them.[81]

I am grateful for the opportunity to work with so many people in order to learn more about myself and make myself better. Life becomes so much more exciting when you see interactions as a way to better yourself and learn attributes of others you do not have. I hope these suggestions will cause you to question your status quo and cause your clients to want to call you.

1. Be Responsive

We as clients appreciate you are busy and have other clients but we expect a response within four hours. Responsiveness does not require immediate answers; acknowledging our request and setting up a time to talk would often suffice.[82]

A simple response lets us know that you will get to it and that we do not need to reach out to another adviser. I once had a boss who had a five-minute window to respond before he looked for someone else for the project. He did not need the work done immediately; he just needed to know it was off his plate and on someone else's.

2. Be Proactive

Do not just respond to our direct question—anticipate issues and ask follow-up questions.

Often we do not appreciate the issues and rely on you to ask us the relevant questions. For instance, Section 332 requires the liquidating entity to be solvent. Before spending considerable time structuring a complex transaction, ask us if the liquidating entity is solvent. Ask us the threshold questions to make sure we can get out of the starting block. Wisdom is not in the answer but in the questioning process.

3. Be Candid

Be willing to tell us your initial "gut" thoughts—we understand it is subject to further thinking and research. There is always a tension of balancing the business realities and figuring out the tax consequences.

Tax is hard—until you put pen to paper and think through all the issues, it is difficult to have comfort that a structure will work from a tax perspective. However, appreciate the tension from our perspective. When the business people are in the idea/negotiating stage, we need to be responsive and we cannot let tax hold up the business deal. We need to quickly identify the risks and proactively advise "our" client on how best to structure the transaction.

4. Be Decisive

Take a position and be willing to defend it. David Ogilvy, referred to by many as the father of advertising, said that there is no shortage of people with brains. "The spinal column seems to be in much shorter supply."[83]

5. Show You Care

Find ways to show us you care about us and not just our "business." Do not be complacent—try to win us each day. For example, send us articles or cases of interests and note why they are applicable, check in, provide us access to the "A" team.

6. Be Thoughtful

Albert Einstein said, "It's not that I'm so smart, it's just that I stay with problems longer." We want to trust you, we will not question your fees.

7. Be a Business Adviser

We do not just want a tax specialist; we want a business adviser. Think outside of your comfort zone. Be comfortable leaving your area of specialty when suggesting ideas.

8. Be Concise

Again, to quote Albert Einstein, "If you can't explain it simply, you don't understand it well enough." Figure out a way to explain issues in a concise manner and leave out unnecessary issues. Be comfortable living with ambiguity.[84]

9. Make Our Problems Your Problems

We expect you to lose sleep at night so we do not have to. Do not leave any stone unturned. Try and appreciate the pressures we are under.

10. Consider the Apple Effect

People love Apple products and find ways to use them more: Make us want to call you because of your brilliance, insights, and energy.

Help us see things differently. We all suffer from change blindness. No matter how many times we look at something it is hard to see it differently than we previously saw it. The key is that we should look at everything we do not as we are accustomed to seeing, but as something new. Help us find ways to look at things from a new angle and new perspective. If you can, like the iPhone or iPad, we will seek ways to engage you.[85]

11. Remove Your Ego

Remove your ego: Perhaps the greatest obstacle to getting into our heads is ego. Ego blinds us to define success by getting what we want instead of helping the other person get what they need. If we experience you as full of ego, you will lose our trust.

When you interact with us, check in with yourself and make sure ego is not the driving force.

For example, we know you are smart—you do not have to tell us. Nonetheless, you should see every interaction as an opportunity to impress us. Marketing is not just for the marketing department.

Conclusion

Too much criticism and confusion, Donald Rumsfeld famously said, "There are known knowns; there are things we know that we know. There are known unknowns; that is to say, there are things that we now know we don't know. But there are also unknown unknowns; there are things we do not know we don't know." I think this quote encapsulates many of the suggestions above and is important to remember as you attempt to climb into our heads.

There are times when we know what we know and we are just looking for you to confirm (be responsive and candid). There are times when we know what we do not know and we need you to educate us, stimulate us, and advise us (be decisive, thoughtful, and concise).

Then there are the times when we do not know we do not know. If this pertains to negative implications, let us know as soon as possible (be proactive) and certainly make sure the issues you raise are valid (do not create issues that only three people in the world would consider—be thoughtful). However, if the unknown unknowns pertain to a positive tax solution, then you are in the Apple space—you have our attention and you have the chance to win a client for life (the Apple effect).

That being said, the funny thing is that playing in the unknown unknown space does not always require a spectacular result, it simply requires you to climb into our head each and every day.

Article 2

More Head Games: Getting Into the Head of the Adviser– How to Be a Good Client

Sam Walton, the founder of Walmart, said, "There is only one boss. The customer. And he can fire everybody in the company from the chairman on down, simply by spending his money somewhere else."

It is an axiom of American business that the customer/client is always right. While undoubtedly true, this maxim does not always reflect how we (the customer/client) feel about the customer-service provider relationship. We spend the majority of our day working and interacting with people; however, many of us feel starved of any purpose, meaning, and relevance. These intangible cravings were the essence of my article, *Head Games: Tips for Getting Into the Head of Your Client*.[86] The intangibles often cost the adviser little in the way of time and effort, yet mean a lot to the client; the client can become "addicted" as a result of these intangibles.

I wonder, though, what role the client should play in building this relationship. Specifically, how can the client help in creating a nourishing and more productive experience between himself or herself and the adviser?

I recently made the transition (and paradigm shift) from being an adviser to a client. In this article, I remove my client hat and reflect on what it was like to be the adviser (although we are all advisers/clients in one way or another to one person or another). With this new perspective, I reflect on what my "best" clients did to enhance the relationship and experience. It is not surprising the best clients had the skill sets to elicit the best work from me and achieve ingenious, creative tax planning. Importantly, in no way do the suggestions below mitigate the responsibility of the adviser to climb daily into the head of the client.

The following advice, I believe, will not only provide a better client experience but should also stretch the impact of every dollar spent on advisers.

1. Be Patient and Be Clear

Creativity is a child of discomfort. Allow your adviser the time to mull over an issue and think about it from as many angles as possible. Your adviser's goal should be to leave no stone unturned. However, it is very important that you be clear on your instructions.

There are times when you want your adviser's quick initial thoughts on an identified issue, and there are other times when you want your adviser to thoughtfully contemplate whether the transaction presents additional (not-yet-identified) issues and, if so, to analyze these issues. There is a spectrum here of how you might want the adviser to proceed; you will help your adviser (and yourself) by stating up front where you want your adviser to be on this spectrum, and telling your adviser if that changes over time.

It is crucial to tell your adviser how involved you want to be in the process.

Moreover, it is crucial to tell your adviser how involved you want to be in the process. Some clients want to be part of the sausage-making process while others do not want to see how the sausage is made and just want the end result (tax wizardry).

2. Be Rescuable

In tax (and life), it is easy to get married to an idea and sub-consciously manipulate the facts to support it.[87] The Talmud states that "A captive cannot release himself from his own prison."[88] A good client is open and accommodating to an adviser's fresh perspective, which may be different from the initial inclination about the right or best way to address an issue.

3. Be Open

Every real estate agent will tell you that the three most important things about real estate are location, location, location. In law, they are facts, facts, facts. Do not over-filter the facts for your adviser—allow him or her to determine what is relevant and to ask for follow-up information.[89]

A great adviser helps develop an analysis or solution that is based on a particular set of facts—understanding the general, abstract principles of the law often is the easier part. It is also more expensive for your adviser to try and uncover facts. Ask your adviser fairly regularly to tell you what he or she thinks the facts are, so that everyone is on the same page. It is all about facts. Wrong facts will cause your adviser to chase the wrong issues and spend more of your money.

A great adviser helps develop an analysis or solution that is based on a particular set of facts

**—understanding the general, abstract principles
of the law often is the easier part.**

It is also important to be attentive from the onset regarding the business/accounting/financial goals or constraints related to the transaction, and to explain these to your adviser. That way your adviser will not spend time coming up with the perfect tax answer, which then may turn out to be impractical or unrealistic. In addition, learning more about the non-tax context for a transaction may actually help your adviser to identify a creative solution that not only works under the relevant technical tax rules but is also relatively easy to justify under common law business purpose or similar principles.

4. Show How Conversant You Are (Or Are Not)

There is a famous scene in *The Godfather* where Michael Corleone is in a restaurant with Virgil Sollozzo and Capt. McCluskey, the crooked police chief. Sollozzo leans over to the police chief and says, "I'm gonna speak Italian to Mike." The police chief says, "Go ahead." As discussed above, part of the job of a good adviser is to educate the client. However, it is imperative that the adviser know whether or not you speak the language (understand the law) or want to speak the language of the particular issue at hand.

Tax can be tough sailing and requires stops at many foreign ports. There are times when the client is in a completely foreign land and has no inclination to learn the language (i.e., the law); however, there are times when the client is fluent in the language but simply needs help with a few new words. Speaking the language also includes tax jargon (e.g., citing to revenue rulings or cases as a shorthand way to discuss an issue without having to unpack it).

In my new role as the client, prior to speaking with an adviser on the phone or in person, I often send an email with the relevant facts, what I think the main issue is and my initial analysis of the law. This greatly decreases the length of the call between me and the adviser and increases his or her productivity. Importantly, the adviser has a sense of how much of the law I know and hence how much time needs to be spent explaining the law to me. This practice also gives the adviser an overview of the important issues right away and gives him or her the ability to consider additional issues/ opportunities (if that is what I want).

The key to showing how conversant you are or are not in anything in life requires you to be vulnerable. Vulnerability is the bridge between mere interaction and authentic engagement.

5. Be Trusting

Albert Einstein said that "Whoever is careless with the truth in small matters cannot be trusted with important matters." Once your adviser earns your trust and shows consistently the high level of skill and diligence that you want to see, believe that the recommendations made to you are the same he or she would make if it were his or her own company. Although each and every day your adviser should try to earn your trust, it is important that you, too, are open to trust and willing to invest the time and effort needed to create a trusting relationship.

6. Challenge Suggestions

Trust your adviser but challenge his or her suggestions if they do not make sense or are overly complex. You adviser is driven to find the best results but does not always consider the pain and complexity of living with his or her recommendations. Even the best specialists can be wrong or have missed something significant, and thus it is important that you not be afraid or reluctant to challenge.[90]

However, it is also important to recognize that, sometimes, there is no silver bullet. You occasionally cannot get a perfect solution to one tax issue without sacrificing something on a different tax issue. Or, it may be the case that a tax issue and a business consideration turn out to be too difficult to reconcile. Sometimes this is the product of an unimaginative or inexpert tax adviser — but sometimes it is just an unavoidable fact. There is an art to knowing when you have pushed the adviser enough, and have gotten him or her to give all the genuinely constructive suggestions possible.

7. Be (Somewhat) Permanent

Appreciate the fact that your adviser knows there are a hundred other advisers who you can hire instead; no one adviser has a monopoly on the law, brain power, or innovation.[91] Your adviser knows this and, as a result, he or she often is afraid to lose you and in many instances may need your business to survive. This is a good thing, from the client's point of view. However, there also can be a benefit in fostering a relationship in which your adviser has the freedom to take some creative risks and not fear losing you.

Most creative individuals (which, yes, does include those in the tax field) are insecure. If the adviser is overly fearful of losing you, he or she may be less able to operate at the most insightful and creative level.[92] If the relationship hits a snag after being very productive, do not be hasty and dismiss your adviser—tell him or her what is wrong and offer the opportunity to fix the problem. Moreover, allow your adviser the freedom to be candid with you. The client-adviser partnership cannot be sustained without candor on both sides.[93]

8. The Google Effect

It has been said that because Walmart's differentiating factor is price, it views Google as its biggest competitor. Why? Google has the power to find products cheaper than those offered by Walmart. Sometimes, tax is a purely commodity-like product where price is the key differentiator —but often it is not. So do not reflexively choose an adviser based on price alone. You would not hire a doctor, architect, or business consultant solely based on a price. Tax consulting is a specialty (an extremely complex specialty) and as with any specialty, it takes at least 10,000 hours of intense practice and hard work to master the subject.[94] Allow your adviser to differentiate himself or herself from other advisers according to his or her unique talents. If you decide to choose your adviser solely on price then he or she is just another commodity.[95] David Ogilvy famously remarked that his advertising agency "hires gentlemen with brains."

9. Seek Judgment

In a must-read article for all tax practitioners, David Hariton provided a brilliant analogy between the posted speed limit on a road and the practice of tax law.[96] The speed limit on a road may be 40 miles per hour but the practice of the local police may be only to pull over those going 60 miles per hour or more. Similarly, Hariton wrote that although a tax position may be technically correct, the judgment of the adviser is necessary to determine how fast the client is driving if the position is taken.

A good client should seek not just the technical answer from the adviser but push the adviser for his or her judgment.

I have been trained to dissect and analyze the law. In a given day, I wrestle with U.S. (and sometimes foreign) tax issues of all types. After substantial exertion, I generally can understand the law as a technical matter. However, as a novice to a particular area of the tax law, my lack of experience at times prevents me from differentiating between a position that is, in practice, too aggressive and one that is overly conservative. A good client should thus seek not just the technical answer from the adviser but push the adviser for his or her judgment.[97]

I routinely ask my advisers the following question: "If the speed limit is 40 miles per hour, how fast or slow I am going?"

10. Be Great

In life, happiness is not just about how much you have; it is about how little you miss. We live in a culture where we believe happiness comes from having more. The legendary founder of Allied Stores, B. Earl Puckett, said, "It is our job to make men and women unhappy with what they have." It takes a great person to avoid falling into this trap. Similarly, in tax, a client should feel secure in his or her decision not to simply always rely on advisers. It is the obligation of the client to strive to become better as a tax practitioner.

We need to constantly improve ourselves. Also, it takes a smart and well-informed client to ask smart questions and bring out the best in his or her adviser (as I noted in my prior article, wisdom is not in the answer but in the questioning process).

11. Give the Adviser Praise

Expect and demand perfection from your adviser and when he or she achieves it, offer praise.

Conclusion

I previously wrote how my daily Starbucks experience provides me with a sense of dignity and respect. This is clearly in large part due to the charisma of the barista but perhaps it is equally, if not more, a result of my expectation of the positive experience. The value of something is not so much its objective worth but in the uniqueness we ascribe to it. Wine in an expensive bottle tastes better than the same wine in a cardboard box.

Similarly, the way you perceive and treat your adviser affects not only your experience but the way the adviser relates to himself or herself. When the optimal client-adviser relationship is achieved, Aristotle explains, "the whole is greater than the sum of its parts." This greater whole (whether due to our role as client or adviser or as both) has the power to unlock greatness on many levels.

My 5 Favorite Business Books

- David Lapin, *Lead by Greatness* (Avoda Books 2012)

- Sam Walker, *The Captain Class* (Random House 2017)

- Adam Grant, *Give and Take* (Penguin 2013)

- William Thorndike, Jr., *Outsiders* (Harvard Business Review Press 2012)

- John Brooks, *Business Adventures* (Open Road 2014, Reprint)

Special acknowledgement: Special thanks to Andreas Apostolides for helping me develop, refine and communicate these insights. Andreas's patience, thoughtfulness and deep thinking inspires me and is a large part of my success.

About the Author

JARED DUNKIN is a finance executive and tax lawyer based out of Washington, D.C., where he lives with his wife and five children. Jared finds joy in mentoring young professionals, many of whom have advanced into senior positions in business and finance around the world. In his younger years, he fondly remembers serving as a Peace Corps volunteer in the Dominican Republic, and some of those early experiences continue to inspire and enlighten him to this day.

Jared can be reached at brasstaxbook@gmail.com.

Endnotes

1 *See Anyone Who Doesn't Take Truth Seriously in Small Matters Cannot Be Trusted in Large Ones Either*, QUOTEINVES-TIGATOR.COM, April 15, 2015, https://quoteinvestigator.com/2014/04/15/large-truth/.Original quote appears to have been made in Einstein's last statement, first published in New Outlook: Middle East Monthly, Volume 1, Number 1, Albert Einstein On Israeli-Arab Relations (Tazpioth, Tel Aviv, Israel, 1957).

2 Peggy Noonan, Opinion: *If Adults Won't Grow Up, Nobody Will: From Facebook to Harvey Weinstein, America's scandals amount to a giant crisis of maturity*, WALL STREET JOURNAL, Apr. 5, 2018, *available at* https://www.wsj.com/articles/if-adults-wont-grow-up-nobody-will-1522970344 (last accessed Feb. 21, 2019).

3 Ray A. Smith, *Why Dressing for Success Leads to Success: New research shows that when workers wear nicer clothes, they achieve more*, WALL STREET JOURNAL, Feb. 21, 2018 (discussing study by Michael W. Kraus at Yale School of Management, described in a Journal of Experimental Psychology article in 2014), *available at* https://www.wsj.com/ articles/why-dressing-for-success-leads-to-success-1456110340 (last accessed Feb. 21, 2019).

4 Matthew Hutson & Tori Rodriguez, *Dress for Success: How Clothes Influence our Performance*, SCIENTIFIC AMERICAN, Jan 1, 2016, available at https://www.scientificamerican.com/article/dress-for-success-how-clothes-influence-our-performance.

5 Quote attributed to a 2014 interview with Complex. See Insanul Ahmed, *TURN THE PAGE: WHEN KENDRICK LAMAR DELIVERED A CLASSIC WITH GOOD KID, M.A.A.D CITY, NOBODY SAW IT COMING. NOW THAT THE WHOLE WORLD IS WATCHING, CAN HE OUTDO HIMSELF?*, *available at* https://www.complex.

com/covers/kendrick-lamar-interview-turn-the-page-2014-cover-story/.

6 John Simons, *'I Lost It': The Boss Who Banned Phones, and What Came Next: Employers limit cellphone use to regain attentiveness. Workers use watches and laptops instead*, WALL STREET JOURNAL, May 16, 2018, *available at* https://www.wsj.com/articles/can-you-handle-it-bosses-ban-cellphones-from-meetings-1526470250 (last accessed Feb. 21, 2019).

7 *The Mere Presence of Your Smartphone Reduces Brain Power, Study Shows*, UT News, June 26, 2017, available at https://news.utexas.edu/2017/06/26/the-mere-presence-of-your-smartphone-reduces-brain-power; see also Nicholas Carr, How Smartphones Hijack Our Minds: Research suggests that as the brain grows dependent on phone technology, the intellect weakens, WALL STREET JOURNAL, Oct. 6, 2017, *available at* https://www.wsj.com/articles/how-smartphones-hijack-our-minds-1507307811 (last accessed Feb. 21, 2019).

8 Kermit Pattison, *Worker, Interrupted: The Cost of Task Switching*, FAST COMPANY, July 28, 2008, https://www.fastcompany.com/944128/worker-interrupted-cost-task-switching.

9 Lolita C. Baldor, T*he Defense Department is adding new restrictions to cellphone use in the Pentagon*, BUSINESS INSIDER, May 22, 2018, *available at* https://www.businessinsider.com/ ap-apnewsbreak-pentagon-adopts-new-cellphone-restrictions-2018-5.

10 For a brief, 3-minute discourse on the significance of going "all in", *see* Gary Vaynerchuk, *GO All IN ON YOUR STRENGTHS*, YOUTUBE.COM, June 13, 2016, available at https://www.youtube.com/watch?v=frXPukkfOiI.

11 Bob Dylan, *It's All Right Ma*, on Album: Bringing It All Back Home (Columbia Records 1965).

12 *See* Tom Monahan, *Around the World in 50 Offices — Shaping the Future of Work*, LinkedIn article, May 17, 2016, https://www.linkedin.com/pulse/around-world-50-officesshaping-future-work-tom-monahan/ ("CEB Real Estate research indicates that workplace quality is one of the largest drivers of collaboration, innovation, and motivation — second only to manager quality.").

13 See chapter #2, *supra, Would you check your cellphone at a funeral? When is it cool to be old school?*

14 *See Happiness Can Spread Among People Like a Contagion, Study Indicates*, WASHINGTON POST, Dec. 5, 2008 (describing a longitudinal study by Nicholas A. Christakis and James H. Fowler, published in a British medical journal, indicating that people who are happy or become happy boost the chances that someone they know will be happy, and that happiness and positive emotions can spread across groups for extended periods), available at http://www.washingtonpost.com/wp-dyn/content/article/2008/12/04/ AR2008120403537.html?noredirect=on.

15 *See* Mike Berardino, *Mike Tyson explains one of his most famous quotes*, SUN SENTINEL, Nov. 9, 2012, http://articles.sun-sentinel.com/2012-11-09/sports/sfl-mike-tyson-explains-one-of-his-most-famous-quotes-20121109_1_mike-tyson-undisputed-truth-famous-quotes. Of course, this quote seems to derive inspiration from the well-known phrase that "no plan survives contact with the enemy," attributed variously to Carl von Clausewitz and Helmuth von Moltke, among others — see *No Plan Survives Contact with the Enemy, available at* https://bootcampmilitaryfitnessinstitute.com/military-and-outdoor-fitness-articles/no-plan-survives-contact-with-the-enemy/ (con-

taining quotations from these two individuals as well as other famous generals and writers on war, and including a list of references).

16 David Ogilvy, *The Eternal Pursuit of Unhappiness: Being Very Good is No Good, You Have to Be Very, Very, Very, Very, Very good* (Ogilvy & Mather Worldwide 2009).

17 This quote has been attributed variously to Albert Einstein, Richard Feynman, and Lord Rutherford of Nelson, among others. See https://skeptics.stackexchange.com/questions/ 8742/ did-einstein-say-if-you-cant-explain-it-simply-you-dont-understand-it-well-en.

18 Quote attributed to Maya Angelou. See Alexandra Petri, *How to misattribute a quotation*, WASHINGTON POST, Dec. 5, 2008, available at https://www.washingtonpost.com/blogs/ compost/ wp/2015/04/07/how-to-misattribute-a-quotation/?utm_term=.6f4bc819831c.

19 Amy Cuddy, *Your body language may shape who you are*, TED, https://www.ted.com/talks/amy_cuddy_your_body_language_shapes_who_you_are/up-next (last accessed Feb. 21, 2019).

20 Michael Nordine, *'Game of Thrones': Littlefinger's 'Fight Every Battle' Speech Was an Insight Into His Mind* — and Advice on How to Watch the Show: Those who underestimate Lord Baelish do so at their own peril, INDIEWIRE, July 31, 2017, *available at* https://www.indiewire.com/2017/07/game-of-thrones-littlefinger-speech-aidan-gillen-1201861961/.

21 "Finding a diamond in a muddy road" is a Zen *koan* (a riddle or puzzle used by Zen Buddhists to meditate in order to unravel hidden truth); see *Finding a Diamond on a Muddy Road*, http://

www.ashidakim.com/zenkoans/2findingadiamond.html (last accessed Sept. 23, 2018).

22 Sukkah 5b.

23 HEADSPACE, https://www.headspace.com/headspace-meditation-app.

24 This quote has been attributed to Harold Macmillan, though apparently never authenticated. *See* Robert Harris, *As Macmillan never said: that's enough quotations*, TELEGRAPH, June 4, 2002, *available at* https://www.telegraph.co.uk/comment/personal-view/3577416/As-Macmillan-never-said-thats-enough-quotations.html (stating that Oxford Dictionary of Quotations included this quote in 1999 as "attributed" to Harold Macmillan).

25 Charles Duhigg, *The Power of Habit: Why We Do What We Do in Life and Business* (Random House 2012).

26 See Carmine Gallo, *Steve Jobs: Get Rid Of The Crappy Stuff*, FORBES.COM, May 16, 2011, *available at* https://www.forbes.com/sites/carminegallo/2011/05/16/steve-jobs-get-rid-of-the-crappy-stuff/#41251b2e7145.

27 As described by Theodore Rousseau, the one-time (and controversial) curator in chief at the Metropolitan Museum of Art, "[w]ith a minimum of colors he uses the maximum of technical means to an extent equaled by few other painters." In addition, while Rembrandt's range of colors was "always astonishingly limited, [] the variety of tone within this range is infinitely rich." *See* Theodore Rousseau, Jr., *Rembrandt*, pp. 84-86, *available at* https://www.metmuseum.org/pubs/bulletins/1/pdf/3258296.pdf.bannered.pdf.

28 Attributed to Albert Einstein, though may not be authenticated.

29 Thomas A. Edison, *The Diary and Sundry Observations of Thomas Alva Edison* (Greenwood Press 1948), p. 110.

30 Daniel Kahneman, *Thinking, Fast and Slow* (Farrar, Straus & Girroux 2011).

31 Jeff Bezos, Founder and CEO, Amazon.com, Inc., 2015 Letter to Shareholders, *available at* https://www.sec.gov/Archives/edgar/data/1018724/000119312516530910/d168744dex991.htm.

32 Alex Banayan, *The Third Door: The Wild Quest to Uncover How the World's Most Successful People Launched Their Careers* (Currency 2018).

33 "Never was so much owed by so many to so few" is the title of a wartime speech made by the British PM Winston Churchill on 20 August 1940, referring to the Royal Airforce's (i.e., the "Few") courageous defense of the British Isles against the German Luftwaffe during the Battle of Britain.

34 See my mentor's LinkedIn page (David Lapin), available at https://www.linkedin.com/in/davidlapin/. *See also* David Lapin, *Lead By Greatness: How Character Can Power Your Success* (Avoda Books 2012), available for purchase on Amazon.com at https://www.amazon.com/Lead-Greatness-Character-Power-Success/dp/0983467706.

35 This quote is attributed to Leonardo da Vinci, among others, though it may not be possible to authenticate.

36 According to Wikipedia, social capital is seen as a form of capital that produces public goods for a common good, has become popular since the 1990s and 2000s, and "broadly refers to those factors of effectively functioning social groups that include such things as interpersonal relationships, a shared sense of identity, a shared understanding, shared norms, shared values, trust, cooperation, and reciprocity." *See Social capital*, WIKI-

PEDIA.ORG, https://en.wikipedia.org/wiki/Social_capital (last accessed Jan. 14, 2019).

37 Taken from the passage: *"The opposite of love is not hate, it's indifference.* The opposite of art is not ugliness, it's indifference. The opposite of faith is not heresy, it's indifference. And the opposite of life is not death, it's indifference. Because of indifference, one dies before one actually dies. To be in the window and watch people being sent to concentration camps or being attacked in the street and do nothing, that's being dead." (emphasis added). According to Wikipedia, this is attributed to an article about Elie Wiesel in the U.S. News & World Report (October 27, 1986); see Elie Wiesel, WIKIQUOTE.ORG, https://en.wikiquote.org/wiki/Elie_Wiesel#Quotes (last accessed Jan. 14, 2019).

38 See https://www.forbes.com/sites/actiontrumpsevery-thing/2014/01/12/you-miss-100-of-the-shots-you-dont-take-so-start-shooting-at-your-goal/#31cac13c6a40.

39 Adam Grant, *Give and Take* (Penguin 2013).

40 Paulo Coehlo, *Eleven Minutes* (HarperOne 2009).

41 Sharon Pomerantz, *Rich Boy* (Grand Central Publishing 2010).

42 Attributed to Winston Churchill — *see Winston S. Churchill > Quotes*, Goodreads.com, available at https://www.goodreads.com/author/quotes/14033.Winston_S_Churchill?page=27.

43 *See* Shahrzad Rafati, *What Steve Jobs taught executives about hiring*, FORBES.COM, June 9, 2015, *available at* http://fortune.com/2015/06/09/shahrzad-rafati-keeping-your-best-employees

44 See chapter #8, *supra, Are you adulting? Churchill vs. the sycophants...*, and note 40, *supra.*

45 *See* chapter #9, *supra, The importance of being Marvin — 3 tips for unlocking your potential.*

46 This refers to an article by Tom Monahan published on LinkedIn on December 1, 2017, titled *With apologies to the Replacements, Pleased to Meet me — see* https://www. linkedin.com/pulse/apologies-replacements-pleased-meet-me-tom-monahan (last accessed Nov. 7, 2018).

47 Definitions of gratitude often cast the term in terms of what was received. For example, Merriam-Webster defines it as "the state of being grateful," which in turn is defined as being "appreciative of benefits received." See "Gratitude", MERRIAM-WEBSTER.COM, https://www.merriam-webster.com/dictionary/gratitude; *see also Healthbeat: Giving thanks can make you happier, available at* https://www.health.harvard.edu/healthbeat/giving-thanks-can-make-you-happier (last accessed Nov. 26, 2018). However, these attempts frequently stumble by focusing on what was received, rather than what gratitude enables. As this chapter explores, gratitude remains one of the most critical tools for forging successful relationships throughout life on an individual level, as well as motivating teams to go above and beyond the call of duty to invest their discretionary energy into their Responsibility and working together, to achieve outsized results. *See* Sam Walker, *The Plymouth Colony and the Business Case for Gratitude: A management lesson from 400 years ago on how to build a happy team*, WALL STREET JOURNAL, Nov. 25, 2019 (discussing the importance of gratitude, recognized by American leaders like William Bradford, George Washington and Abraham Lincoln in "dark, challenging times", who used it as an effective and must-have tool to "heal divisions, lift morale and build resolve by fostering a spirit of thankfulness", and mention-

ing how some companies use routine opportunities to express gratitude to colleagues as a tool to (i) enable employees to feel vulnerable and emotional, and thus build a sense of trust, (ii) improve communication, and (iii) place greater emphasis on what makes customers happy), *available at* https://www.wsj.com/articles/the-plymouth-colony-and-the-business-case-for-gratitude-1543162842?tesla=y (last accessed Feb. 21, 2019).

48 See chapter #5, *supra, Finding a diamond in a muddy road — what is your creative space to play?*

49 Victor Frankl, *Man's Search for Meaning* (Pocket Books 1984), pp. 16-17.

50 *See infra* note on Harvard Study of Adult Development.

51 See Robert Waldinger, *What makes a good life? Lessons from the longest study on happiness*, YOUTUBE.COM, Jan. 25, 2016, available at https://www.youtube.com/ watch?v=8Kk-KuTCFvzI&feature=youtu.be ("Good relationships don't just protect our bodies; they protect our brains[.]"). For more information on the Harvard Study of Adult Development, *see* Liz Mineo, *Good Genes are Nice, but Joy is Better: Harvard study, almost 80 years old, has proved that embracing community helps us live longer, and be happier*, THE HARVARD GAZETTE, Apr. 11, 2017, https://news.harvard.edu/gazette/story/2017/04/over-nearly-80-years-harvard-study-has-been-showing-how-to-live-a-healthy-and-happy-life/ (discussing the Harvard Study — one of the world's longest studies of adult life — which found that close relationships are more essential to, and a better predictor of, happiness throughout life than any other element, whether money, fame, social class, IQ, or genes; starting in 1938, the Harvard Study tracked 724 Harvard men over 75 years and some of the most disadvantaged boys in Boston's tenements).

52 See Jennifer Breheny Wallace, *How to Raise More Grateful Children: A sense of entitlement is a big problem among young people today, but it's possible to teach gratitude*, WALL STREET JOURNAL, Feb. 23, 2018 ("Ms. Cormier says that she has worked hard to make gratitude a family habit since her children were little—and now it has become the norm. She encourages finding gratitude in the **'everyday stuff,'** she says, not just in response to birthday and Christmas presents. She also tries to teach gratitude by example. When her children help out around the house, like noticing when the trash is full and taking it out, or holding the door open, she thanks them. And now, she says, 'my kids thank me every single time I put fresh sheets on their bed,' chaperone a field trip or make them dinner.") (emphasis added), *available at* https://www.wsj.com/articles/how-to-raise-more-grateful-children-1519398748 (last accessed Feb. 21, 2019).

53 See supra note 53.

54 See chapter #7, *supra, How many doors do you see? The joy of what can be….*

55 The expression was popularized by John Lennon in *Beautiful Boy (Darling Boy) in Double Fantasy*, the seventh and last album released by Lennon during his lifetime ("Before you cross the street take my hand. / Life is what happens to you while you're busy making other plans."). *See Beautiful Boy (Darling Boy)*, WIKIPEDIA, https://en.wikipedia.org/wiki/ Beautiful_Boy_(Darling_Boy) (last accessed Jan. 14, 2019). However, a nearly identical quote is attributed to Allen Saunders, creator of the dramatic comic strips "Mary Worth" and "Kerry Drake"; it has been traced to the "Quotable *Quotes*" section of the January 1957 edition of Reader's Digest, though the original cartoon has not been found. See garson, *Life is What Happens To You While You're Busy Making Other Plans*, QUOTEINVESTIGATOR.COM (MAY 6,

2012), https://quoteinvestigator.com/2012/05/06/ other-plans (last accessed Jan. 14, 2019).

56 See, e.g., *Discount Airline Pioneer Herb Kelleher Dies; Founded Southwest*, BLOOMBERG (Jan. 3, 2019), https://www. bloomberg.com/news/articles/2019-01-03/herb-kelleher- co-founder-of-southwest-airlines-has-died-at-87 (discussing Kelleher's focus on his people, and the fact that "[h]e treated everyone the same: with respect", in addition to starting the industry's first employee profit-sharing program); see also Press Release, Allied Pilots Association Lauds Southwest Founder Herb Kelleher for "Putting Employees First" (Jan. 4, 2019), available at https://www.alliedpilots.org/News/ID/6583/Allied-Pilots-Asso- ciation-Lauds-Southwest-Founder-Herb-Kelleher-for-Putting-Em- ployees-First (quoting APA President Capt. Dan Carey as saying of Kelleher, "When you put employees first, they're motivated to make your customers happy. And when your customers are happy, most likely your shareholders are too. The result is a virtuous cycle that benefits everyone involved.").

57 This story is partly retold in Robert Spector, *Blake Nord- strom: An Appreciation* (Jan. 4, 2019), THEROBINREPORT, https://www.therobinreport.com/blake-nordstrom-an-apprecia- tion (last accessed Jan. 14, 2019).

58 *See* Douglas R. Conant, *Secrets of Positive Feedback*, HARVARD BUSINESS REVIEW (FEB. 16, 2011), https://hbr. org/2011/02/secrets-of-positive-feedback (discussing impor- tance of creating a personal connection early on with team members, looking for successes to celebrate, and writing handwritten notes to build goodwill); *see also* Douglas R. Conant & Mette Norgaard, Touchpoints: *Creating Powerful Leadership Connections in the Smallest of Moments* (Jossey-Bass 2011).

59 *See* Leadership Principles, https://www.amazon.jobs/en/principles (stating with regard to Frugality: "Accomplish more with less. Constraints breed resourcefulness, self-sufficiency and invention. There are no extra points for growing headcount, budget size or fixed expense.") (last accessed Jan. 14, 2019); *see also Amazon's Jeff Bezos continued to drive a Honda long after becoming a billionaire – and it reveals why he's so successful*, BUSINESS INSIDER (Jan. 19, 2018), https://www.businessinsider.com/jeff-bezos-honda-reveals-reveals-why-hes-so-successful-2018-1?r=UK&IR=T

60 Christine Porath, *Why being respectful to your coworkers is good for business*, TED, https://www.ted.com/talks/christine_porath_why_being_nice_to_your_coworkers_is_good_for_business?utm_source=linkedin.com&utm_medium=social&utm_campaign=tedspread#t-888173 (last accessed Feb. 21, 2019).

61 *See* chapter #3, *supra, Are you a "What's Up" or WhatsApp kind of person?*

62 See chapter #12, *supra, Superhuman Fuel: Recognizing the Good.*

63 As far as I know, the "84%" statistic is unsupported by research and provided here solely for the reader's entertainment.

64 See chapters #5 (*Finding a diamond in a muddy road — what is your creative space to play?*) and #12 *(Superhuman Fuel: Recognizing the Good), supra.*

65 See chapter # 8, *supra, Are you adulting? Churchill vs. the sycophants.*

66 *See Fernando Cueto — Puerto Plata hervía por tumbar a Trujillo: Uno de los Líderes del Movimiento 14 de Junio en esa Provincia Narra a Listín Diario los Pormenores de la Organización, Sus Integrantes y Acciones*, https://listindiario.com/la-republi-

ca/2010/06/11/145742/puerto-plata-hervia-por-tumbar-a-trujil-lo (last accessed Feb. 21, 2019) (Don Fernando is shown seated in the center of the photograph accompanying this article). Reading this article many years later, I also realized that Don Fernando was one of the heroes of the Dominican 14th movement. *See 14th of June Movement*, https://en.wikipedia.org/wiki/14th_of_June_Movement (discussing Fernando Cueto for his role in leading a group of female guerillas, who were "under the direct control of the committee and specifically of Fernando Cueto, and included among others Aída Arzeno, Ana Valverde viuda Leroux, Argentina Capobianco, Italy Villalón, Elena Abréu, Carmen Jane Bogaert de Heinsen and Miriam Morales) (last accessed Feb. 21, 2019).

67 "Campesino" generally refers to a native of a Latin American rural area, and especially, a Latin American Indian farmer or farm laborer; *see* "Campesino", MERRIAMWEBSTER.COM, https://www.merriam-webster.com/dictionary/campesino; for a non-scholarly, yet in some respects informative discussion of how campesinos in many geographic locales have been subjected to "marginalization, exploitation . . . and restricted (or no) access to land," *see also A Word About the Word Campesino*, HEIFER.ORG, https://www.heifer.org/join-the-conversation/blog/2012/April/a-word-about-the-word-campesino.html (last accessed Feb. 21, 2019).

68 Andrew Beaton, *Who's in the Atlanta Falcons Owner's Huddle?: Much like when he ran Home Depot. Arthur Blank looks for blunt feedback, including from James Dimon*, WALL STREET JOURNAL, Feb. 2, 2019, *available at* https://www.wsj.com/articles/whos-in-the-atlanta-falcons-owners-huddle-11549083616 (last accessed Feb. 21, 2019).

69 See chapter #2, *supra, Would you check your cellphone at a funeral? When is it cool to be old school?*

70 Sarah Begley, *Lady Gaga Says Her Public Persona Is a 'Separate Entity' from Her True Self*, TIME.COM, http://time.com/4361123/lady-gaga-stefani-germanotta-true-self.

71 *See Persona*, WIKIPEDIA.ORG, https://en.wikipedia.org/wiki/Persona (last accessed Feb. 21, 2019).

72 Bill Murphy Jr., *Tom Brady Says the Same 4 Words to Every New Player on the New England Patriots, and It's Pure Genius: Imagine you're a new player in the NFL, and you meet Tom Brady. Here are the four words he'll say*, INC.COM, *available at* https://www.inc.com/bill-murphy-jr/tom-brady-says-same-4-words-to-every-new-player-on-new-england-patriots-its-pure-genius.html (last accessed Feb. 21, 2019).

73 Andy Puddicombe, *All it takes is 10 mindful minutes*, TED, https://www.ted.com/talks/amy_cuddy_your_body_language_shapes_who_you_are (last accessed Feb. 21, 2019).

74 Check out Puddicombe's website, HEADSPACE, *available at* https://www.headspace.com/headspace-meditation-app, which provides details on the app and includes helpful articles on the topic of mindfulness (last accessed Feb. 21, 2019).

75 Amy Cuddy, *Your body language may shape who you are*, TED, https://www.ted.com/talks/andy_puddicombe_all_it_takes_is_10_mindful_minutes (last accessed Feb. 21, 2019).

76 Permission to use this analogy was granted by Glen on the non-negotiable condition that I mention that "this so-called 'mentor' and his wife are voracious readers of, and enriched by" by ideas in this book "to the point that it calls into question who is the mentor and who is the mentee."

77 Rudyard Kipling, *If, available at* https://www.poetryfoundation.org/poems/46473/if--- (last accessed on Feb. 21, 2019).

78 Kazuo Ishiguro, *The Remains of the Day* (Vintage *International* 1988), at p. 29.

79 Research backs up the benefit of doing things on a *continuous* basis (i.e., without interruption), for while doing things in fits and starts (i.e., *continually*) accomplishes nothing, doing things continuously actually changes patterns in your brain.

80 The philosopher Plato said, "the beginning is half of ev-erything" («αρχή δε το ήμισυ παντός»); his student Aristotle one-upped him quipping that "the beginning seems to be more than half of the whole" («Δοκεί γάρ πλείον ή ήμισυ παντός είναι η αρχή»), a play on the meaning of *"archē"* (αρχή) as both first principles and as a starting point of deductive reasoning. Cf. Aristotle, *Nicomachean* Ethics 1098b.7, H. Rackham transl. (Harvard Univ. Press, 1926).

81 The author gratefully acknowledges the insightful comments of Paul Laino, a colleague at Discovery, in compiling the list of suggestions.

82 After law school, I worked for a top law firm. The office lore was that the head partner, a top Washington, D.C., power broker, received thousands of emails a day and he did not go to sleep at night until he responded to all emails. Whenever I sent him an email (with much anxiety), he would respond within sec-onds. Obviously my e-mails were not of significant importance but I believe he recognized my apprehension and out of a sense of tremendous kindness he would quickly respond. Former col-leagues at both the law firm and accounting firm often confided in me how destroyed (irrelevant) they felt when they would pour their life into a project and the partner would not respond for weeks. This could easily be avoided with a simple email say-ing "thank-you for your hard work—I need time to digest it."

83 David Ogilvy, The Eternal Pursuit of Unhappiness/Being very good is no good, you have to very, very, very, very, very good (Ogilvy & Mather Worldwide 2009).

84 A must read for all advisers is Bayless Manning's famous and courageous 1982 article on the need for less ambiguity in law. Bayless was a former tax partner at Paul Weiss. See Bayless Manning, Hyperlexis and the Law of Conservation of Ambiguity: Thoughts on Section 385, 36 Tax Law 9 (1982). See also Richard Lipton, "We Have Met The Enemy And He Is Us": More Thoughts on Hyperlexis, 47 Tax Law 1 (1993).

85 Philip Wagman, a tax partner at Clifford Chance US LLP, is an excellent example of the Apple effect. Wagman also exemplifies the ability to transition between tax, legal, and business considerations.

86 Jared Dunkin, Head Games: Tips for Getting Into the Head of Your Client, (1 DTR J-1, 1/3/11).

87 In psychology, the term "cognitive afterimage" is used to explain the concept of why we get stuck in patterns of viewing the world and how, unfortunately, the patterns from our professional lives spill over into other areas of our lives. For instance, lawyers are trained to be critical thinkers; however, this pattern of seeing the world can have negative consequences outside of work. See Shawn Achor, The Happiness Advantage (Crown Business 2010).

88 Talmud, Berachot 5b.

89 I remember as a junior lawyer going to a partner to give him a report on the facts and issue of a matter. The partner stopped me and spent the next hour drilling me on the facts. I kept telling him the requested facts were irrelevant. I was wrong.

90 Terence Cuff, a prominent tax lawyer and prolific writer in the area of partnership law, writes that with respect to partnership agreements, "there should never be a presumption of correctness, regardless of how powerful the law firm, how many offices are on its letterhead, how many former Supreme Court clerks the law firm employs, or how impressive the practitioner who prepared the venture agreement—or how many pages the venture agreement consumes—or how prettily it is typed." See Terence Floyd Cuff, "A Personal Perspective on Drafting Partnership and LLC Agreements," in Practicing Law Institute, Tax Planning for Domestic & Foreign Partnerships, LLCs, Joint Ventures & Other Strategic Alliances (2006).

91 Of course, there are those people of rare ability who in addition to being really smart have the special "it" factor—they understand how the world really works. With respect to advisers, there are also those advisers with the rare ability of truly caring about you and not just your business (i.e., your money). They show it by buying shares in your company, using your products, and behaving as if they are members of your team.

92 My hero, Einstein, seemed to value the intellectual firepower necessary to play in the world of tax. For instance, Einstein once admitted that the reason he had to hire a tax adviser was because "This [tax] is too difficult for a mathematician. It takes a philosopher." Einstein also said that "The hardest thing in the world to understand is income tax."

93 My point that the client should be somewhat permanent is much different from preserving status quo as it is crucial not to be content preserving the status quo with your advisers (and with yourself as a leader). Not only does the desire and false comfort of status quo blind you to obvious problems, it inhibits innovation and prevents free choice. With free choice, each

interaction provides for a number of possible outcomes and possibilities.

94 Malcolm Gladwell, Outliers: The Story of Success (Little, Brown and Co. 2008).

95 To some extent, there is a trend toward commoditizing tax work as a result of advisers selling work based on capped or fixed fees. A lot of the compliance function of tax is a commodity. However, when it comes to tax planning and mitigation of risk, an adviser normally requires significant tax expertise, experience, and judgment. The best advisers also consider non-tax issues such as operational and legal considerations. When considering the price of different advisers, consider also the value of what you are getting.

96 See David P. Hariton, The Frame Game: How Defining the 'Transaction' Decides the Case, 63 Tax Law. 1 (2009).

97 Judge Mary Ann Cohen in Esmark v. Commissioner, 90 T.C. 171 (1988), said it best by calling tax an "art." In Esmark, the government tried to recast a transaction it did not like. At the time of the transaction there was a special exception to Section 311 (it turned it off) that allowed a subsidiary's stock to redeem the stock of its parent corporation. Judge Cohen stated in her decision, "This is a challenging case. We must decide the primary issue under the rule and principles in effect at the time of the transaction despite historical criticism and subsequent abolition of that rule. To do otherwise, would be to undermine tax planning as an essential ingredient of business decision-making (and as an art)."

Made in the USA
Middletown, DE
05 November 2020